Medic Up
Vietnam Veteran's Memoir
Charley J. LaFontaine

Radical Women

Foreword by Paul Lavelle, CMSgt, USAF, (Ret), MSC
Founder and Advisory Board of Operation Restored Warrior
www.operationrestoredwarrior.org

Cover and Interior Design by Lisa Bell DBA Radical Women
www.bylisabell.com

Radical Women
PO Box 782
Granbury, TX 76048
www.bylisabell.com
email: LisaBell@bylisabell.com

Paperback ISBN: 978-1-965561-14-0
eBook ISBN: 978-1-965561-15-7

*To my Lord and Savior, Jesus Christ
and for my family. May you always feel his presence.*

Contents

Acknowledgments

Even dedicating this book to Jesus Christ, I must acknowledge Him first. When I look back at the many times I ignored, even made fun of Him, He refused to abandon me. If He ever left me, I wouldn't be here to write this book, and I know that without a doubt. Even in the toughest times of life, He was always there—even when I didn't know it or see His hand.

To my beautiful bride, Blanche. Without your encouragement, typing skills, and continued support, I might never have finished getting my stories from my brain onto paper. You walk with me daily, listening, understanding, and giving me more love that I deserve. I am more than grateful to have you beside me in the best of times and the not-so-great ones. Thank you for taking a chance on me and loving me for the last thirty-one years.

For my beautiful daughters, Callie Ann and Shana Rene, who complement Blanche and myself perfectly. I wrote this primarily for you and to preserve a little of our family history.

Paul Lavelle, founder of Operation Restored Warrior, I treasure our friendship. All you do for veterans encourages me to press forward and continue the ministry God gave me to walk alongside many who struggle with the past.

Last but not least, Thank you, Lisa Bell—writer, editor, and publisher. I met Lisa early in this process and quickly realized we could partner in this project. She supported me with constant encouragement and expertise to start and finish this endeavor. Beyond editing and helping bring this book to publication, I am thankful for the friendship Blanche and I now enjoy with her. Thank you for all your work to improve my stories and assist me in all aspects of finishing this book. Without you, I'm not sure it would have ever gone beyond an idea.

To all my fellow veterans and their families who read this book, may God use it to touch your heart and help you overcome whatever holds you back from all He has planned for your life. Our country owes you a debt it can never repay.

Foreword
by Paul Lavelle

Why would a global movie and television icon like Kelsey Grammer stand on a stage at the Museum of the Bible in Washington, D.C. to champion the healing of veterans? What could possibly bridge the gap between a big Hollywood star and a combat warrior? To answer that, we have to look back more than 18 years to a snowy mountainside in Colorado—and to a man named Charley LaFontaine.

My own journey to that mountain began in the 1960s, watching the Vietnam War unfold on a flickering black-and-white television in Portland, Maine. As a young boy, I watched the evening news tally the casualties like routine sports scores. I saw my brother's friends get drafted. I saw some never return, and others returned as shadows of the boys they once were. Those images stayed with me through my 26-year career in the United States Air Force, where I eventually reached the rank of Chief Master Sergeant. Though I reached the pinnacle of the enlisted ranks, I carried a quiet burden: a feeling that because I served during a long stretch of "peacetime," I hadn't truly "served" like the Vietnam veterans I idolized. It wasn't until after my retirement in 2001, and a life-altering encounter with Jesus on a mountain in Colorado in 2003, that I realized my greatest mission was still ahead of me.

In 2004, I began working with the team at Ransomed Heart Ministries led by bestselling author John Eldredge. It was there I saw the powerful "spiritual component" of warfare. I watched military suicide rates climb and realized PTSD wasn't just a clinical diagnosis; it was a wound of the heart and soul.

In 2008, I was told something prophetic from John Eldredge. "Paul, I don't believe Ransomed Heart can hold the glory of your life."

I was being called to a larger story and a specific rescue mission for my fellow veterans. In August 2008, I founded Operation Restored Warrior (ORW) with a simple but radical conviction: Jesus can completely heal the heart of a warrior. But every mission needs a "plank owner"—a first attendee to test the waters. My search for that first warrior led me to a man named Jack Rogers, a salty, angry Vietnam battle-hardened LRRP Ranger veteran who didn't trust anyone.

He told me, "Call my friend Charley. If Charley goes, I'll go."

That was my introduction to Charley LaFontaine. Charley had served as a combat medic in 1966—one of the bloodiest years of the Vietnam War. Unlike the defensive Jack, Charley had a contagious, full-body laugh that radiated joy, albeit guarded joy. He was kind, yet he carried the weight of the horrors he'd seen while trying to save lives in the jungles of Vietnam. Charley agreed to come, he convinced Jack, and the very first "Drop Zone" was born at Yarmony Creek Ranch located in the high Rocky Mountains of Colorado.

That weekend, Jesus showed up in a way none of us will ever forget. I watched as the Great Physician reached into the decades-old wounds of these Vietnam heroes and began to do the miraculous. Charley wasn't just a participant; he was the proof of concept. He was the evidence that no matter how much time has passed, and no matter how deep the trauma, restoration is possible.

Since that weekend with Charley and Jack, ORW has helped save thousands of lives. We discovered that the "heart wounds" of the infantry soldier to the elite special operator, from the Private to the General are often the same wounds carried by the civilian—the childhood betrayals, physical and emotional abuse, the silences, and the shame. This realization is what eventually led Kelsey Grammer to our Drop Zone. The same healing Charley found as a medic in the mountains was the same healing Kelsey found for the tragic losses in his own life.

Charley LaFontaine is more than a friend; he is a pioneer. He was the first to trust a retired Chief and the radical idea that we could move beyond "clinical coping" and into "complete spiritual healing." As you read Charley's story in the pages that follow, you aren't just reading a biography of a Vietnam veteran, you are reading the story of a man who had the courage to face his past so he could help pave the way for thousands of others to find their future.

Thank you, Charley, for trusting me—and more importantly, for trusting Jesus—with your heart. You made it easy for me to ask, "What else is possible?"

With Deep Love and Respect,
Paul

Paul J. Lavelle
Chief Master Sergeant, USAF (Ret.), MSC
Founder, Operation Restored Warrior
Rescue, Rebuild, & Restore

First ORW Drop Zone: (Left to Right) Paul, Charley, Jack, and Ken

Introduction

ON JULY 4, 1966, a Continental Airlines jet landed at Tan Son Nhut, the only major air base in the country of South Vietnam. We had arrived. Alongside 211 other FNGs (freaking new guys), I disembarked for our one-year tour of duty. We came to save Southeast Asia from the domino theory of Communism engulfing all the countries aligned with South Vietnam.

Looking through the small window of the plane, we saw many individuals moving like ants in the 108-degree temperature. As the door opened, a powerful wave of heat hit our faces, and an overwhelming stench hit our nostrils—worse than a dead alligator in a Louisiana swamp in mid-July. This sweet, pungent odor of the dead and dying would surround our lives for the entire tour of duty and beyond.

We exited the plane onto the waiting buses with much anticipation. Why was there chain-link wire sealed over the windows of the bus? We dared ask.

"To keep hand grenades from being thrown into the bus," stated one of the Marine guards providing security around the perimeter of the airfield. "We had three killed and eight wounded in a mortar attack last week, and they had only been in country approximately fifteen minutes." The Marine's face never shifted during his explanation.

Several other guys checked their watches while I checked mine.

After the initial shock, my thoughts drifted to the medic's duty and purpose. In essence, the medic was primarily to "conserve the fighting strength" and save as many of the wounded and dying as possible. Regardless of how many appeared before you with immediate needs for medical treatment to survive their wounds.

I couldn't help wondering at the same time. How many of the wounded could he save in those fifteen minutes? How serious were the injuries of the wounded? How many of them survived and went on with life, or made it, only to die later?

Before we left the bus, the heat zapped my strength, and I became very thirsty. All FNGs, including me, were prodded forward to begin processing so we could get to our assigned units.

They called me "Medic Up" and "Doc." During my tour of duty, few used my name.

After Vietnam, I returned home every bit as wounded as if someone threw a hand grenade in the bus that first day. Only some wounds don't show up in a physical way. And many of mine took root long before I left for Vietnam.

Charley's Birth

WE SAT ON MAMA'S bed as she explained how proud she was of me. She spoke of a special love for her firstborn as she looked at the pages of my "Baby Book." The book contained details, notes, and even a golden lock of my hair she had cut and attached to a page. That moment was a confirmation of my mother's love for me.

October 2, 1946 was a rainy, cool, and very dark night in the little Gulf Coast town of Bay St. Louis, Mississippi, according to her. Mama shared that at age seventeen, her time in labor was the longest eighteen hours she ever spent in her birthing bed.

She had pictures of the Hardy Court Government Housing Project we lived in then. We stayed there until we moved into the Live Oak Subdivision behind the Gulfport Veterans Administration (VA) Hospital. We lived there when she shared that special memory with me.

Our house had two bedrooms and one bath (maybe 1,000 sq. ft.) with a floor furnace—a government-issued (GI) financed home. Mama explained she and Dad had lived in Hardy Court Housing since my dad returned from WWII, and then I was born. We moved to our present house when I was about two or three years old, after the VA Hospital hired Dad as an orderly at the high-end salary of $23 a week. Our house note was $49 a month. This special loan saluted his service as a paratrooper during the war.

Seeing and hearing her explain the past did not help me connect the dots of my life.

Of course, at nine years old, I said nothing to Mama about my uneasiness from the previous formative years I had lived until then. I did not relate to the past my mother described during this visit until now. She made it sound normal.

My first memory was having my face rubbed in spilled milk on the tray of my highchair. I sat in that highchair while Mama threw something at my dad. She later told me she threw a glass ashtray at him.

As she spoke, I seemed to remember experiencing more physical pain during those years. But these thoughts slipped quickly away to a boy starting the first grade at the Northeast Ward Elementary School in Gulfport, Mississippi. I spent the next six years growing and having all the fun of living on the Mississippi Gulf Coast. Like the gifts of sandy white beaches, salty gulf waters, and the delicious seafood which abounded for all the families living within its reach.

Nice memories—if they happened. A trip to the beach was not for us, because we would get sand in the car—a 1949 Plymouth he treated like a "limo."

First grade was not that eventful except for learning, for some unknown reason, that I was different. I mean profoundly different. For example, most of my classmates' parents attended the PTA meetings, but Dad had only come to the school once during my first-grade year (at enrollment). During that onetime visit, he told the principal to introduce me to the paddle if I needed it and to make sure to inform him of my misbehavior. He would finish the job at home with another spanking as soon as I got home.

The worst part of the experience was not what he said, but the way he said it.

"I want you to tear his ass up if he doesn't behave and phone me at 5422J (party line phone number), so I can tear it up some more."

The sad part was that other teachers and students heard his request. Embarrassing at best. Did they take him seriously? I never tested them to find out.

The second and third grades continued in the pattern of uneventfulness—except for my ears, my poor self-esteem, and the pain of not having any friends.

Mama said they pulled my ears outward when using the doctor's forceps during my birth. Whatever the reason, I gained several hurtful nicknames such as "Taxi Cab Doors" or "Dumbo the Elephant's Friend." During this period of growth, I was introduced to team sports like baseball, but softball more often. The athletic kids picked the best players for their teams, and of course, they chose me last or next to last. I lacked their level of athleticism. At that time in my life, I didn't know the expression, "What doesn't kill you, it will make you stronger." Either way, nothing stopped the hurt and pain for the seven-year-old boy.

I was very young when my dad taught me, "Your best friend is a dollar."

There would be no overnight sleepovers with friends, no friends for dinner (either at another's house or having a guest), and no birthday parties. Dad told me birthdays were just another day, and if your mom made you a birthday cake, you needed to feel thankful. He concluded these were our marching orders for life, but at seventeen, I discovered something different.

At age seventeen, I began connecting the dots about the right way and the wrong way to live.

Living with my dad was like living on an "island" with one man ruling all of us whom he kept captured there. Along with his family, my dad was trapped in his "short man syndrome" and his need for complete control.

This awakening to living on an island meant a seven-year-old in the third grade recognized a harsh reality. His family was not cut from the same pattern as the families of any other boy he knew at school. His environment closed all of them off from the outside world. They viewed even the closest neighbor across the street from a distance. Not the way a normal child lives.

To clarify for my readers (especially my daughters, Callie and Shana, whom I will introduce later), I will attempt to explain the years of life on the "island."

A typical weekend, starting on Saturday morning, went like this. Our 7:45 nightly bedtime spanned seven days a week, with no exception on Friday evenings. Young and energetic, I awoke early after going to sleep before the sun went down. We had a standing and present rule for this time of the day. Dad did not permit us to get up except for a trip to the bathroom followed by a return to our beds.

We learned to put items in the bedroom the night before to entertain ourselves until we had permission to get up. My sister, Darlene, and I shared a small 10' x 11' bedroom with a tiny closet. Half of it belonged to her, and I got the other half. Set up military style by the sperm donor, he made us keep clothes split up.

Everything in the house was cramped, but we had a massive yard. It needed space to include a septic tank.

I always checked out as many books as allowed from the school library, so I entertained myself with obsessive amounts of reading. It filled the time until told I could leave the bedroom. Only he could set the exact time for us to move to the breakfast table. The worst case was if the "old man" decided to sleep in until 9:00 a.m. or later. This restriction was pure torture for two young children who woke up hungry and alive, eager to greet the day!

Even as a young child, I thought of him as the "old man" and not Dad. I would call him a lot worse things in the years to come—even until his death at 86 on Veteran's Day, November 11, 2010. Yet I always respected him for who he was—my sperm donor. He lost his "parent card" very early in my life on his island.

I did attempt to discuss this island life with him on different occasions throughout my adult years. But his basic answers accused me of only dreaming these days of emotional and physical pain and confusion. (And here I am with my sound memory, writing this smorgasbord of mixed emotions. Desiring to put the truth in writing. I feel compelled to do so for my loved ones—Mama, my sister, Darlene, and my younger brother, Steve.)

Now, writing about my sister, Darlene, would encompass my writing another book about our lives together. I will share windows of our times together on our island with Mama as brother and sister against the world of pure ignorance.

Darlene and I had a brief existence together due to our parents' divorce, which happened when I was 13 and Darlene was 11. We had small amounts of time together and didn't get along during our lives on the island where the sperm donor ruled. Darlene remained attached to Mama, and I stuck to the sperm donor.

Looking back, the most common time we had was every Saturday morning after our bowl-of-cereal breakfast. We had to ride our bikes over two miles for me to learn Latin, so I could become an altar boy. Not that I wanted that position, but at that age, I didn't defy my father. Besides, we both attended catechism classes until almost noon and then rode our bikes back home. The weather provided the most difficult part of this weekly endeavor. Good, sunny, and hot or bad, cold, and rainy, we had to ride our bikes to the classes. No one ever drove us that I can remember.

Of course, the sperm donor worried more about wasting his gas and oil than any concern about our safety or comfort. This also became his reason for no school sports. Don't forget his refusal of going to the beach. Besides wasting oil and gas, we might get sand in the car—an unforgivable offense.

Every day, we took separate baths immediately after arriving home from school, which was approximately 3:15 to 3:30 p.m. Before the sperm donor arrived home from work around 4:30 p.m., we had to complete all our homework.

We submitted to our daily regimented routine on the island. But Linda Darlene, referred to as Darlene, and I, nicknamed CJ, were doomed from the beginning.

Every summer, my parents sent me to my grandparents' home in Picayune, Mississippi. I never knew what Darlene did while I was gone, but I didn't care. The time with my grandparents gave me a taste of freedom and some sense of normalcy—unless they displeased the sperm donor.

I didn't see it then, but as a child God gave me those summers with my grandparents so I had some foundation of knowing about Him. He was with me even then.

The Whippoorwill Sings

BEFORE I WENT TO bed every night, my mom prayed with my sister and me. Because it was the 7:45 p.m. nightly routine for 365 days of the year, it was a beautiful ending to our day.

Now I lay me down to sleep, I pray the Lord my soul to keep. If I should die before I wake, I pray the Lord my soul to take.[1]

There was an amazing bird I listened to as I lay there in bed those long evenings, waiting for sleep to arrive. The bird sang his song endlessly. No break, no wavering his song comforted me. It sang for me almost every night.

I decided to go to the library to find out more about this bird and discovered it was a whippoorwill. He was my friend who sang me to sleep most every early sleepless night.

I learned the whippoorwill sleeps on the forest floor or on a horizontal log or branch. They also like leafy woodlands, which surrounded our house. For the record, I looked long and hard to find a whippoorwill next and succeeded.

At that time, the whippoorwill was listed as an Eastern Whippoorwill (Antrostomus Vociferus). There were issues for its longevity due to climate change and other things like removing the leafy woodlands. Often heard but seldom observed, the whippoorwill had an observer who decided to count the rapid chants and counted 1,088 given rapidly without a break.

Then we moved from Gulfport, Mississippi to Biloxi, Mississippi. After that move, I never heard another whippoorwill. I missed my dear friend and comforter who sang to me endlessly at my bedtime—one far too early for an active young boy to sleep. God provided that beautiful melody from the small bird so I could sleep.

Without the song, I struggled and longed for the reprieve of summer with Grandma and Arzo (my step-grandpa). They didn't make me go to bed early. Instead, we all sat and watched the 19-inch black-and-white TV until bedtime (usually around 10:00 p.m. Of course, we never told the old man about that.

In the song of the whippoorwill, Jesus' voice comforted me, although I thought it was only a bird, not Him.

Mama's Gone

OUR MOM WAS THE best—one bright part of my childhood. But today, I clearly understand, with some reservations, why she left.

The final day of life with Mama in our home arrived early on a Sunday morning. My EF (Earth Father) woke me about 3:00 that morning to wait with him for her to return home. He had a loaded pistol (9 mm German Luger he acquired and brought home as a paratrooper after WWII). He was in one of his violent moods and told me he was going to shoot whoever let her out of his or her car. We waited, my eyelids fluttering with sleepiness but not daring to close.

Around 7:00 a.m., she came in from an all-night escapade. I'm not sure who brought her home that morning. Apparently, the driver did not let her out where he could see, so she was walking down the street toward the house. She looked and walked like someone who had been drinking—a lot.

Upon her entrance, EF had her sit in a chair in the living room. Then he went and woke up my sister and brother and had us sit on the sofa facing her. He asked her if she intended on staying with him and helping raise us or taking to the streets, drinking alcohol all night—or whatever she was doing on a regular basis. (I called it her escape mode.) My sister, Darlene, at age 11, and my baby brother, Steve, at age 5, waited with 13-year-old me. I eyed the pistol with no idea of what to expect.

She replied, "If I stay, do I have to sleep with you?"

"You GD right you do."

With only a second's hesitation, she walked over to the sofa and kissed each of us, muttering, "I'm sorry."

Then she walked out the door. I didn't see Mama again until we reunited when I was 25 years old!

With my young understanding, I assumed she could no longer tolerate his history of creating hardship for all of us. He never changed, but it didn't take long before he found another woman who somewhat erased his daily attitude of anger and pain.

In the long run, she became more mentally ill than he was. She ruled over him in many of the same ways he abused Mom. As for myself, I started working jobs that allowed me the pleasure of being outside the negative life they both lived and created for themselves.

Soon after that day, I realized Mama had alcohol issues, and we lost her to the addiction. We buried her when she was only 53. Even though I understood Mama's addiction, I lived in denial of my own alcohol issues. Didn't have my mama then, didn't have my sister then, and EF only added to my reasons for drinking. I'm glad I finished my tour and came back a survivor instead of a victim of the war. I didn't know the Lord back then, although He kept me alive all that time. And I was unaware Jesus was always there with me.

However, Jesus Christ redeemed and brought me into the light on June 24, 1985. In 1988, through my six-year-old daughter, I became a true believer in His grace and wisdom. With today's issues, at 78, I continue seeking His face and His will for me and not doing my will except to be available mostly for the Afghanistan and Iraqi veterans seeking peace and learning "the story and the ending" for each of us.

As far as Mama leaving, like I said, I didn't see her from age 13 until age 25. When I was 25, she contacted me and gave me the impression she was near death's door.

She lived in Denver, Colorado, but I went to visit at Christmas and reunited with Mama and somewhat with my sister.

She didn't die then. The entire thing was a ruse to get me to Denver. And it worked—I went.

For more than 30 years after Mama finally passed, I didn't see my sister, Darlene, until she came to Granbury, Texas from Burnsville, Minnesota in 2022 to visit and celebrate my birthday. I'm so thankful we reconnected then. Now, we talk often. So, we made the circle complete between my sister in her 70s, my brother in his 60s, and myself at 78. Nevertheless, I found out you can't be a sissy growing old.

In all of it, Jesus was with me.

After Mama

AFTER LEAVING, MAMA TRIED several times to get visitation rights, so she could come and see us, maybe take us to a movie. However, I guess you could say my earthly father had me brainwashed into a state of almost hating her.

Darlene refused to accept his daily structure and rituals any longer. Eventually, he put her in a Catholic convent in Covington, Louisiana. In 2022, I found out my sister spent two years there before Mama rescued her, and then she raised my sister in an Air Force family. By the time she had custody of Darlene, Mama had married an airman.

When Mama left, because I was the oldest, I became the "ginnywoman," which meant I became a bottle-washing, dinner-cooking, and clothes-washing maid. There wasn't an electric dryer, so I washed the clothes at night and got up with the first light to hang them on the clothesline. Back then, most people had washing machines. But a quality set of poles with a cord stretched between them and an ample supply of wooden clothespins allowed the sun to dry everything from socks to bedding.

The neighborhood women talked to each other across the clotheslines, but I was too embarrassed. They might see me hanging out the clothes, and the thought rushed heat to my face if I even considered the possibility. I also had to keep the yard up, making it look presentable to match the neighborhood. In the summer months, that included keeping it mowed.

Steve, not quite old enough for school, needed help in the mornings. I had to get him up and ready to stay at a childcare home while Darlene and I went to classes during the school year. Come around 3:00 p.m., I started dinner to have it ready when the earth father came in at 4:30 p.m. Although Mama left, he still expected his food on the table when he came in from work. During that time, he also left me in charge while he went on what I call a date night. Whether it included an actual date, he went out and often came back inebriated—flat-out drunk several times.

One afternoon, when he came home at his usual time, I was bringing the clothes for the day in from the clothesline to fold and iron. He told me to come into the house, because he wanted me to meet my new Ma. I went into the house to meet this woman, Eloise.

Over time, she displayed abnormal behavior, becoming mean and downright cruel—like a witch with three brooms. For example, she lied to my earth father, saying we misbehaved when we did nothing wrong. We got in trouble, and she watched the punishment. He always believed her and never questioned the made-up stories.

Regardless of my internal hopes for her to disappear, they ended up marrying each other, but not before they had a date night that ended up in a bad car accident on Highway 49. (By then, we no longer lived behind the VA Hospital in Gulfport, Mississippi and had moved several miles up to a subdivision in Biloxi, Mississippi.)

Anyway, he didn't come home one night. We went over a week without any knowledge of his whereabouts. Then someone came to the door and knocked.

"Hey, kid. I'm Doyle E.—Eloise's oldest son."

I simply stared at him.

"Are you aware your dad and my mother were in a serious auto accident?"

I shook my head. "No. I don't know where he is."

"Mom went through the windshield. She's at Memorial Hospital." He paused before adding. "They took your father to the VA Hospital in Biloxi."

At least I knew he hadn't died, although the son offered no real help for our situation. I shared that we were out of everything. No milk, no bread, and we didn't have any money. He gave me my EF's room number and said the EF told him to tell me to come see him.

We lived about four or five miles from the VA Hospital. The son didn't offer to take me, so I ended up walking.

In the past, I had several experiences walking along the beach there. Various birds flew over and defecated on me almost every time. Then I had to walk through a neighborhood where kids threw rocks at me. So, I didn't look forward to that long hike at the whim of a heartless man.

But I made it to the vet side of the VA Hospital, only for him to tell me he needed me to find the car where they had the accident. He insisted I get his German P-38 (the one he brought back from WWII) out of the glove compartment. And he gave me $20, if I remember right—enough to get some bread, milk, and a few other things for us. Twenty dollars went a lot farther back then, but it had to feed three of us until whenever he made it back home. I left the hospital on foot and walked back home after finding the car, retrieving the gun, and taking a trip to the store.

As a sidebar, our 17-inch TV went out, so we had no entertainment except for reading. I always loved to read. But raising Darlene and Steve when we were home for the summer had numerous challenges. As I mentioned earlier, Darlene and I went to school, came home, and did our homework. Then I cooked dinner and cleaned up the kitchen while EF got ready to go out—at least before he met Eloise—nothing short of that. He expected me to take care of all the things

Mama did before she left. At 13, I had little choice in the matter.

After they got married, he couldn't afford the house payment. The house went back to the mortgage company at that point. He had been working for 23 years at the Gulfport VA Hospital, and that is where he met Eloise.

When I was 16, we moved to Jackson, Mississippi. They were supposed to have jobs waiting for them at the VA Hospital, but that didn't happen. We moved to a new place, and then they were both unemployed. I managed to get a job bagging groceries at a Kroger food store 10 or 11 miles from our new place. Although I got some tips, the minimum wage in the 1960s was 80 cents an hour. Every day, I hitchhiked to the store and back home. As a student with limited availability for working, I made about $23 a week.

Eventually, Earth Father went to work for Pepsi Cola. After a three-day turnaround, he was back home, unemployed. Eloise took a $200 per month job at the public hospital. To hear her tell the story, they hired her as the director. I doubted it, considering I made almost half that much at my part-time job.

Still in the US Army reserves, EF had access to C-rations, which is what we lived on when I was in the 10th grade. When my birthday came around on October 2, 1963, President Kennedy had put a Special Forces Reserve into place. On my 17th birthday, my earth father took me with him to his National Guard Unit. I took the military oath as a soldier in the US Army, which was a six-year hitch with the Special Forces Reserve.

I was supposed to graduate high school in 1964 and then head off to boot camp at Fort Polk, Louisiana. After boot camp, the plan was for me to attend jump school. Once I finished jump school, I'd do six years in the Special Forces Reserves. I didn't hesitate or question the plan. At least I'd be out from under his direct orders.

After we left Jackson, Mississippi, but before I graduated, he finally obtained a position at the US Public Hospital in New Orleans. After 26 years in the system, he left with a retirement as a GS2.

Even then, Jesus was with me and had a plan for my life, but I didn't know it.

Arzo and Grandma

I EXPERIENCED THE BEST times of my life (excluding current days and the births of Callie and Shana) while living with Grandmother Madge and Arzo. These summer visitations lasted until the end of my childhood at age 13.

Arzo Sneelgrove was my step-grandpa, but he treated me like a son. He and Grandma had no children. He worked as a lumberjack or logger, which resulted in a permanent injury that prevented him from fathering any children. Maybe that was the reason he treated me like his blood son.

He taught me so much about country living without the creature comforts of the cities of Gulfport and Biloxi. He was way ahead of his time—a homesteader before anyone thought it cool.

We lived on an 85-acre self-contained tract of land. With no running water, we manually pumped by hand all the water we used, including a #2 washtub to set all day in the sun for my evening bath. We had a smokehouse for the yearly pig killing in the fall. With good weather, families came to help butcher some of the pigs, producing the primary cuts of pork such as hams, bacon, and hog-head cheese. I never acquired a taste for the cheese, and I kind of felt bad killing the hogs after feeding him throughout the summer and other special school holidays during the year.

So no running water, no indoor plumbing, which meant no bathroom—only the outhouse. It sat quite a distance from the cinder-block house (shotgun style) with a concrete floor that felt like ice during the winter months.

Only one heater, located in the kitchen area, kept us warm. We ate all fresh food from the two gardens we planted yearly. Our saving grace was a tractor I enjoyed driving as Grandpa taught me how to use the implements, like the disk and plows, for creating rows in the garden. One of my main chores, since everyone earned their keep, was a morning and evening walk a good distance from the house to harvest the fresh vegetables. We grew tomatoes, squash, cucumbers, and more. When the field peas and butter beans were ready to harvest, everyone picked tubs full for shelling. Many evenings, we shelled until 8 p.m., because Grandma wanted to can them in mason jars for winter meals.

The cow produced all the fresh milk and cream a person could desire, and that included enough to churn butter. The chickens produced all the eggs we needed, and sometimes, I could give some away to neighbors or friends who didn't have chickens.

If we were planning on having a fried chicken dinner, it had to be on Sunday only. Not sure for the reasoning behind that, but one time Grandma served a fried-chicken dinner on a weeknight. Grandpa threw the entire platter of chicken all the way down to the front door. Of course, the platter broke, and the chicken flew in every direction.

He said to Grandma, "Woman, never serve fried chicken except for Sunday dinner."

However, do not be deceived, because Grandpa had his ways. They worked for him. I lived to see Grandma pass at age 88, and because of Grandpa's ways of life, she was well taken care of. We all knew Grandpa saved half of everything he earned and purchased timber tracts throughout North and South Mississippi. He gave Grandma $20 a week to pay the electricity bill and buy groceries on Saturday—a lot back then.

Grandpa would not allow "air bread" in the house, which was "white bread." Grandma prepared a minimum of two large pans of fresh homemade biscuits every day for all bread needs. If you wanted homemade jelly and fig jam to put on a biscuit, she kept them in a screened food pantry with room for all the food we wanted. We had a tiny refrigerator we used mostly for dairy and some meat items.

When I lived there all summer, I had so many fun things to do. Just being away from the sperm donor felt like a haven—a free environment where I thrived. We ventured out, picking berries for homemade jams and jellies, and they were so plentiful. Blackberry, huckleberry, and mayhaw down by the creeks grew in abundance, with freedom to harvest as much as you could. The only scary part was always looking for snakes who also enjoyed the creek and hiding in the bushes. Grandma would take flour, eggs, and milk and bake a cake, then use Mayhaw berries in the icing. I can almost taste it now.

I'm unsure of the direct relationship, but Grandpa was of Indian descent and had a harsh life growing up. However, he had a heart of gold and taught me so much.

As he grew older, his primary health issues involved his breathing. He smoked a lot and rolled his own cigarettes with Prince Albert tobacco. Grandma dipped Garrett snuff until she passed.

I believe I will see them again when I pass from this earth. They were the greatest a boy could claim as his grandparents, and Grandma was the most spiritual woman I ever knew.

Jesus lived on those 85-acres with us, although I didn't know Him then or suspect He walked with us there.

Crash with Bread and Chickens

ONE EVENING, MY OLD man came home from work. We were out of bread, so he gave me money to buy a loaf of bread from the store, close to a mile from our house.

I hopped on my bike and headed out. When I approached a large hill, I tried to ride up, but it proved too much of an obstacle. So, I got off the bike and walked up the hill, pushing my bike with me. Coming back, I hesitated at the hill. Too steep to ride up, I figured going down would be easy. I made my decision, and rode the bike down, holding the loaf of bread, not having to pedal but just coasting.

Without pedaling, I went faster and faster, gaining speed while my heart raced in competition with the wheels. Losing control, the bike went flying off the road, but I fell off while holding the loaf of bread so my body or the ground wouldn't smash it. Smashed bread would earn punishment, and I made sure that didn't happen.

With no serious injuries, I ignored the minor scrapes, picked up the bike, and finished my ride home. I didn't tell anyone what happened. Miraculously, the crash didn't destroy my bike.

At 10 or 11, another incident happened on a Saturday afternoon. The old man seldom allowed bike riding for fun. After completing all my chores on Saturdays, he allowed me to ride—if he was in a good mood. I always hoped for a mood that provided that bit of freedom. I tried my best to please him every Saturday, increasing the likelihood I'd get to ride my bike.

One day, I worked hard all morning, waxing his car, making it gleam enough he'd let me go. While I rode around the neighborhood, I met the leader of the neighborhood gang of boys. He always had comic books and the best bike out there, which indicated his family had plenty of money. Affluent, he naturally became the neighborhood leader.

He said, "Let's play chicken."

For anyone who never played this daring game, chicken involves two people—a person on his bike at one end of the block with the other at the opposite end. Both waited in the middle of the street, hearts pounding and palms sweating. On the agreed signal, we raced our bikes toward each other, never veering from the middle of the street. We dared each other to chicken out and avoid a severe head-on crash. Most of the time, one swerved at the last minute.

I'm not sure why, but that day, I intended to win, since he challenged me. I never had the guts to call him out and challenge such a powerful force among boys. Facing the neighborhood leader, I couldn't quit. For once, I wanted to come out on top.

Speeding toward each other, I didn't chicken out. Neither did he. I suppose we both figured the other one would swerve, but neither gave in to the urge. The head-on collision tore up both bikes, me losing most of the spokes on my wheels. Neither Johnny nor I sustained any serious injuries from our foolishness.

I pushed the bike home, regretting my stubbornness and wondering what to expect. Outraged, my old man asked what happened. I told him Johnny Dennis rode his bike into me. Because the old man could tell, I didn't dare to lie—at least not completely. However, I left out the part about the crash coming from a game of chicken, hoping that kept me from punishment.

It gave my old man an excuse to sell my bike, but he included my sister's bike, too. Needing money to keep us in food, clothing, and shelter, he found a junk man and traded the two bikes for cash.

I won the struggle against Johnny and stood a little taller in the neighborhood. But not without a high price.

I look back at both days involving my bike accidents and realize how badly the crashes could have injured me. Safety helmets didn't exist back then, but if they had, we couldn't have afforded them. Even then, Jesus had His eyes on me, and I never saw it.

Slippery Milky Way

IN GULFPORT, MISSISSIPPI, WE lived in the Live Oak subdivision. Since we had no public-school buses, the parents went to the Gulfport municipality. They advocated for the transportation of elementary students. Children in grades one through six received ten cents for bus fare every day. We had a nickel for getting to school and a nickel to bring us home.

I paid the money and rode the bus each morning, so I didn't show up late for my class. But I kept one nickel and walked home. That way I could stop at the store and buy a large candy bar. In those days, candy bars were enormous. On a particular day, the sun beat down on the pavement, heating everything in its rays. I ate my Milky Way candy bar in small bites to make it last for the entire long walk home. Not yet summer, the temperatures soared that afternoon.

I followed this routine all the time, but for the first and only time, a horrible thing happened. My stomach started cramping about halfway to the house. Alongside the cramping, I desperately needed a bathroom. Stuck in the middle of the road between home and the store, I faced a decision—return to the store or try to make it home. Fighting the pain, I struggled onward, but diarrhea reared its ugly head.

I lost every bit of that candy bar, along with the remains of lunch—in my underwear and leaking out into my pants. I didn't look behind me, certain drops of the mess followed me.

When I got home, I was crying after completely soiling myself. Embarrassed, I feared the old man more. He wouldn't care if it happened beyond my control. I entered the house, cringing and wondering if I could somehow keep anyone from knowing.

My mom met me at the door, hugged me, and told me not to worry. She cleaned me up before the old man got home. My sister didn't find out either—if she did, she kept the secret safe.

That ended my journey of eating candy bars on the way home for fear of another unpleasant incident happening.

Mom didn't tell my old man a lot of things. She tried to protect us when possible, not wanting to give him reasons to punish us. When he went to National Guard meetings once a month, we got to stay up late watching TV, and she gave us peanut butter and marshmallow sandwiches. He never allowed late nights or treats after dinner. None of us shared what went on while he went to the reserve meetings, and we looked forward with anticipation to the next time he left.

Those weekends provided a pleasurable reprieve from the constant restrictions forced on us by the old man. Without them, I'm not sure any of us would've survived his tyranny.

Despite Mom's faults, she showed us a semblance of the way Jesus loved us, although I didn't recognize it during my childhood.

Saturday In-Home Detention

IN THE 1950S, MY sister, Darlene, and I shared a bedroom. Despite having bathed after school, each night before going to bed we followed a mandatory routine. At 7:45 p.m., we washed our legs and feet in the bathtub before being in bed by 8:00 p.m. sharp. No exceptions.

The sperm donor was a regimental commander for the entire household, including my mom. An 8 p.m. bedtime seemed impossible because I was not sleepy. But that was our problem, not his.

We were not allowed to get out of bed except for using the bathroom, and we only had one of those. He usually allowed us to "get up" around 8:30 to 9:00 a.m. on the weekends. I seldom slept that late, especially because of the early bedtime.

When I awakened on a Saturday morning, I read library books until I could get up. My sister interrupted with a whisper as she had nothing to do. We did not have a TV yet, so I did a lot of reading—even after our allowed wake-up time.

Upon getting up, we ate cereal of some type—whatever was in the pantry. Then, for myself, I needed to get dressed to work in and around the house. No staying in pajamas, lounging around, or playing. Darlene and I alternated every other week in dusting the entire inside of the house.

After taking care of the indoor chores, I went outside and reported to him for my next duty orders. Which normally meant washing and waxing his car—a two-tone green and cream 1949 Plymouth sedan. I avoided this weekly endeavor only if it rained, so I prayed for rain.

Whenever we went anywhere in the car, I held tight to my possessions. An old license plate and car mat covered a hole in the floorboard on my side. Though hidden, I knew that hole existed, and losing anything through it would be my fault—disregarding that his car had a hole between me and the road.

He found projects around the house (like taking all the screens down from the windows) meant specifically for me. We had no air conditioners, so we had a window fan. He wanted to make sure all the window screens were clean, so he assigned the duty to me.

Sometimes, when he and I completed his projects on Saturday, I had permission to ride my bike around the neighborhood. Oh, what sweet freedom for me. Out from under his scathing eyes and harsh commands, I sailed along the streets, for a moment forgetting the reality of my home life.

One Saturday, while riding my bike through the neighborhood, Johnny Dee happened to be on the street I was riding down. Johnny was the king bully of the neighborhood. My entire age group (somewhere between eight and ten years old) cowered in terror before him. The sight of him in the road almost made me prefer the chaos of home. Almost.

Johnny and his buddies (Bobby and Danny) started throwing large railroad rocks at me. As I tried to escape, one rock hit me square in the back of my head. I arrived home, bleeding and crying as I entered through the back door.

Sperm donor wanted to know what happened. I explained to him.

He asked, "What did you do?"

"I came home."

"Why didn't you fight back?"

"Because you told me not to get in fights."

"No. I instructed you not to start the fight but to finish it."

In reality, I didn't fight back for fear of what would happen—with Johnny and at home.

However, at that point in my life, I understood my marching orders. That night, as I lay in bed, I made a plan to even up the score with the three bullies that attacked me. Even at my young age, I couldn't count on my dad to stand up for me, and I didn't consider looking for Jesus to avenge me. Maybe He gave me the retaliation idea, although I suspect He wanted to see how I responded instead.

The lunch-pail fight worked better than I imagined.

Lunch-Pail Fight
With Johnny Dee

WITH MY CLEAR UNDERSTANDING of marching orders, at approximately age ten, I proceeded in making a plan to retaliate for the attack with the railroad rocks from that Saturday evening.

In the following couple of weeks, walking home from the bus stop into the neighborhood, I found Bobby and Danny one at a time. I beat the hell out of them with my fists. Their mothers called Mom and wanted to know why I beat up their precious angels.

I really don't know what the mothers discussed with my mom, and frankly I didn't much care. They started this fight as a bully threesome, and I intended to finish it. But I had one person left.

Johnny Dee.

I didn't have to wait long. Johnny sent word out through the neighborhood. He wanted to meet me under the big oak tree at the intersection of the neighborhood's main streets. With strict orders entrenched in my mind, I showed up.

All the neighborhood kids, or so it appeared, gathered to watch what happened. He told me he was going to beat me up for hurting his buddies.

By the way, we could not afford to buy school lunches, so we ate peanut butter and jelly, baloney sandwiches and egg sandwiches, or tuna on Fridays. As good Catholics, we couldn't eat meat that day, because it was a sin to eat meat on Fridays. To this day, I'm not sure why anyone considered meat eating a sin, but we dared not argue the point.

I had a Kit Carson lunch pail, which I was super proud of—one of the few treasures in my otherwise dismal childhood.

As instructed by the sperm donor, I told him to try beating me up. He threw the first punch and hit me upside the head with his fist. I remember only two things after he hit me. One, I almost bit his entire left cheek off. He carried the mark on it for months. Second, as I left the fight, I had only the handle of my lunch box left in my hand.

From that day on, I ruled the neighborhood. No more bullying from Johnny Dee or anyone. It lasted until we moved to Biloxi, Mississippi after my 13th birthday.

Many people might say Jesus wouldn't want us to fight—that we should turn the other cheek. While that may be true, I also think He doesn't like bullies who always hurt others. Somehow, he gave me the strength to defeat my enemy that day and perhaps spare other kids Johnny picked on. I sure didn't see Jesus during that fight, but how else can I explain the victory? Whether I saw Him, someone sure empowered me and my lunch pail.

The Vacant Lot

WE LIVED IN THE Live Oak Subdivision from early in my life. Before my tenth birthday, I acquired enough friends to play cowboys and Indians—like we saw on the 17-inch black-and-white TV. We received only three channels and walked across the room to change the channel. We had to share telephone lines with the neighbors because few, if any, people had private phone lines. Our phone number was "5422J." People listened in on each other's phone lines whenever anyone called, and we all knew it. I inject this factual information because of the following story that affected all the neighbors—because of my playing with matches.

EF was at work, and Mom gave me permission to go out and play. Summertime with no school, I headed outside about 9:30 or 10:00 a.m. As I shared earlier, free time came rarely at our house, but despite my excitement, none of my friends were around to play with me.

What could I do with my free time that morning?

I discovered some matches in the outside shed, and I thought it was a bright idea to build a campfire before I rode off into the woods. We always played as either a cowboy or an Indian. Finding myself alone, I took on the role of the Lone Ranger—without Tonto. After I built my campfire and ate an imaginary meal, I put out the campfire and rode off into the woods.

I don't remember how much time I spent playing on the trails among the thick trees before returning home. When I exited the woods, not one but two city fire trucks with full crews surprised me. They worked diligently to extinguish a fire in the vacant wooded lot between our house and the neighbor's. With the entire wooded area aflame, the fire consumed trees, filling the air with smoke and the scent of a massive bonfire. Worse yet, the fire was spreading behind our modest frame house, to the neighbors' homes, and moving to the houses surrounded by the woods. I'd never seen a forest fire, but the sweltering flames crackled as they licked up trees and continued growing, much like I pictured a forest fire.

Did this all happen because of my campfire?

Apparently, I had not doused it as well as I thought. Shaking, I wondered if we'd lose our home all because of my carelessness. Although scared of that possibility, the punishment I might receive terrified me.

Finally, a few hours later, the firemen arrested the fire without it damaging any homes in the neighborhood. Only through God's mercy, although I didn't understand it then.

I didn't mean to cause a fire, but that didn't matter. This accident created one of the worst summers I spent with the EF.

He got on the phone and told everyone who would listen he was looking for a reformatory school to put me in. Of course, with the party lines, that tidbit of gossip spread through the entire neighborhood.

I truly believe he would have placed me in one of those schools if his seeking produced any fruit. None existed that he could find, though.

I didn't know it then, but God was with me—even in the smoke, raging fire, and aftermath.

Kneeling on Rice

My dad never hesitated to discipline us for any major or minor infraction. Around him at home, we treaded carefully, never sure what he might consider breaking his rules—some he made up on the fly and we knew nothing about. We sure didn't ignore the ones we knew.

For example, he never allowed us kids to speak at the dinner table unless spoken to. Most nights, we ate in total silence, finishing everything on our plates regardless of whether we liked it, had an appetite, or felt sick. Breaking these cardinal rules of silence or failure to eat all the food brought swift punishment.

Always prepared, Dad used his belt to give me a whipping for whatever he thought I deserved it for. My innocence of the perceived infraction didn't matter. He considered any attempt at justification as sassing him, which meant extra licks.

He often gave me a whipping because I didn't complete my homework before he got home at 4:30

p.m. I could have one math problem left or an overabundance of homework that day. It mattered little in one of his reasons for punishing me. It seemed like he took pleasure in using that belt on me.

Around the age of nine or ten, enduring a whipping as I lay across the bed, the belt broke because I would not cry. I lost track of how many licks he administered, but in my stubbornness, I refused to give him the pleasure of my tears.

But the hits I already endured didn't satisfy him.

When the belt broke, he had me get an old newspaper and spread it in the dry bathtub. Then, he sent me into the kitchen where we kept a jar of rice.

He said, "Pour the rice and spread it across the newspaper."

Confused about his intent, I did as told, hoping the punishment would end soon.

Satisfied, an evil smirk covered his face. "Now, take your pants off, get in the bathtub and kneel on that rice for ten minutes."

Again, I obeyed, thinking no problem. Ten minutes kneeling on rice—easy. Until a minute passed, the rice digging into my knees, sharp pain shifting me back on my heels.

I jerked at the boom of his voice. "Add another five minutes."

"What?"

"On your knees. And if I catch you sitting back on your heels, I'll add another five minutes every time."

I returned to my knees.

Adding to the pain of kneeling on rice, he sneaked around the corner periodically, trying to catch me resting on my heels. He added another five minutes to the punishment if he caught me off my knees for even one second. Never knowing when he might appear, I stayed in position as long as possible. Putting weight on one to rest the other only increased the pain on the supporting knee.

Perhaps I should have cried during the whipping. Yet with every minute the rice dug deep, I refused to let tears flow, fighting them back and detesting my dad more. Because I wouldn't cry, he continued this form of punishment, trying to break me.

Once I finally completed the kneeling time, which grew to an hour occasionally. I had to put every grain of rice back in the jar, including the ones stuck to my knees, and replace it on the kitchen counter. For hours following the punishment, my knees ached, covered with angry redness.

Once I got into high school, my old man found more interest in taking my paycheck as punishment for whatever he decided I did wrong. Kneeling on rice finally ended.

Although I never appreciated the harsh punishment, it served me later in life. I didn't know it, but God prepared me to take a lot of pain at nine years old, a forerunner for harsh pain I experienced during the Vietnam War.

Charley J. LaFontaine, Jr.
Vietnam 1966-1967

OCTOBER 2, 1963—20TH SPECIAL Forces Group D, Jackson, Mississippi, and in 1964, New Orleans, Louisiana, Special Forces Reserves

June 3, 1964—U.S. Army Regular, Boot Camp Basic Training, Fort Polk, Louisiana (North Fort)

August 1964—Advanced Training Combat, Fort Sam Houston, Medic, San Antonio, Texas for ten weeks

October 1964—Operating Room Technician (91D20) School, Fort Sam Houston, San Antonio, Texas

November 1964—On-the-Job Training (91D20), Fort Gordon, Georgia

January 1965—Permanent Duty Station, Hospital Company, Fort Ord, California

July 4, 1966—Arrived for Tour of Duty in Vietnam attached to the 173rd Airborne Brigade, 3rd MASH through **January, 1967.** Then reassigned to the 9th Infantry Division as a Line Medic and Convoy driver for a two-and-a-half-ton truck from War Zone D with a twice weekly average of 80 miles one way to Mỹ Tho and Đồng Tâm.

May 27, 1967 to September 30, 1969—Continued in service until honorably discharged from the U.S. Army upon completion of the required six years (1963-1969).

Charley's In-Country Processing Story

ARRIVING IN THE COUNTRY, at the only airbase (Tan Son Nhut) in South Vietnam, at 9:55 a.m., July 4, 1966, we shuffled to the door to exit. The heat—114 degrees in the shade—and stench left us staggering as we offloaded.

The MPs walked around asking individuals what was in their duffel bags as they checked for soldiers smuggling weapons into the country.

Then an MP approached me. "What do you have in your duffel bag?"

"All I have in there is what they issued to me—and a jar of Skippy Peanut Butter."

He looked at his buddy MP. "We have a smart-ass on our hands here." He turned back to me, barking orders. "Dump your entire bag into this bin."

I pleaded with him not to make me do it, thinking about the difficulty of repacking the duffel bag.

His tone grew harsher. "Dump it!"

He found the jar of peanut butter and walked away, realizing I had no guns. After repacking my duffel bag, we proceeded for verification of a ration card for cigarettes and alcohol.

From there, they shuffled us to an area for a verbal introduction and welcome by a Command Sergeant Major (CSM). He verbalized that our arrival thrilled the government, but no one should feel important about being there. Since the government had computed that every man there would produce on average 3.5 children, if you should go down, ten more could take your place. Most of all, nothing had changed since basic training. That meant—do what you're told, when you're told, how you're told with no explanation. He pointed his baton to a row of flag-covered caskets lined up as far as we could see down the runway. He assured us we would not end up like that if we followed orders.

From there, we transferred to buses with windows surrounded by chain-link wire. Being an FNG (Freaking New Guy), we wondered why the chain-link wire covered the windows. An MP explained it prevented hand grenades from being thrown into the bus. The buses dropped us off at the GP (general-purpose tent).

On the way to Tent City A (Repot Depot) was a staging area for each soldier to be sent straight to his unit. We all carried our DD214 (a soldier's entire military history to date). Being stationed at Fort Ord, California, veterans coming back from their tour of duty informed us not to get tagged for a detail. They set them up for "shit details," and you would not go to your unit for ten days if they tagged you.

I went straight to my unit, avoiding the dreaded tag for a detail. Jesus gave me that grace, although I didn't acknowledge Him or ask for His mercy at the moment.

The Village of Mỹ Tho
(Beyond Saigon 1966-67)

As shared earlier, I arrived in the country of South Vietnam (Nam) via jet on July 4, 1966, and survived until May 27, 1967. Then, I returned to the land of the Big PX (Post Exchange) for my discharge from the Army to civilian life.

During my tour in Nam, I served with two major units in the role of a medic. I served approximately seven months with the 173rd Airborne Brigade about 40 miles north of Saigon. It was called the Village Bien Hoa (pronounced Ben Wa). This unit was a firebase behind the Bien Hoa Airbase that was in the process of being built, and I was assigned to the 3rd Surgical Hospital to support the men of the 173rd. My time spent with this unit comprised performing various types of surgery on the wounded. I have many stories of wounded and dying soldiers.

Mỹ Tho village was an 80-mile drive from War Zone D. The village of Bien Hoa, which is where I was stationed until my attitude of "rage" not "anger" decided to mouth off to the Command Sergeant Major.

Fatigue set in rapidly with a multitude of surgeries on the half-dead and many dying on the operating room tables. Four different operating rooms stayed filled most of the time. I figured out a better path for myself. I learned and mastered the surgical instruments and techniques needed to work with a specialized group of vascular surgeons. These types of surgeries consisted primarily of reconnecting the arteries. We performed many brachial arm and femoral leg artery bypasses to avoid amputating the limbs of these men. The average time to perform each operation required an eight-hour window, depending only on the severity of the wound.

Examples: They never assigned me to a new case without confirmation of any vascular cases but immediately placed me on any vascular case determined in pre-op (before surgery). But most of all, I had new friends, "officers," to socialize with during off time. Better yet, I enjoyed drinks at the Officers' Club. I belonged to the NCO Club since I ranked as an E-5 Sergeant (Specialist E-5). The code was definitely NO fraternizing with the officers.

I didn't know it, but this position and title took me up the ladder with the doctors and nurses that controlled this special team. So I became special—one of a kind, if you will. This created safe zones for me. Also, a death trap because of a transfer as a punishment by the Commanding Sergeant Major to the motor pool attached to the 9th Infantry in the Mekong Delta.

Let me explain the death trap transfer assigned as punishment by the Command Sergeant Major (CSM) of the 173rd Airborne Brigade.

Prior to being assigned to the 9th Infantry by the CSM, I must inject the fact of serving in what we call today "the old army." This had not changed from 1964 to 1966 for the daily military command to do what you were told, when you were told, and how you were told—with no explanation. CSM told me several times, which in his man's army (Korea) meant trouble, not to fraternize with the officers. I had been going to the Officers' Club although we had the NCO club. Fraternizing with the officers afforded me the privilege of socializing with people like Henry Fonda and Martha Raye. The army invited them to the Officers' Club for cocktails on their "handshaking tour." NCOs didn't get that honor. CSM kept telling me to stop fraternizing with the officers.

To quote him, "In his man's army, there was not to be nor would there be any fraternizing with the officers." I ignored him to my detriment.

After seven months of his BS, I talked myself into "special orders," which included my being cut from

Brigade and reassigned to a 9th Infantry Aid Station. I had to acquire a license to drive the 80-mile convoy twice a week, driving a two-and-a-half ton truck (military fuel). We used diesel, but the trucks were so new they could run on oil and gas. All trucks had 55 mph governors on them to keep them slow enough for the militia snipers, taking one to three men at a single attack on the convoys. For the reader's information, my rank was E-5, a buck sergeant specialist NCO (Non-Commissioned Officer).

The catalysts for my transfer to the 9th Infantry came from two major issues. My demise began when "Westy," General Westmoreland, who I rated on a scale of one to ten. I would have given him a zero for having a second Full Field Inspection. He created two individual inspections for us at the 173rd Airborne Brigade during my months of serving there. The general was arriving the next day for a Full Field Layout of each soldier's equipment.

Sewing on arms and legs to prevent amputations, I had worked my way up to the Thoracic Team with Dr. Levensky, attached to the 3rd MASH (Mobile Army Surgical Hospital). I must inject this was nothing like the *MASH* program shown on TV. I just saw enough of it to know they created the program to entertain the war protesters and draft dodgers in Canada and Jane Fonda's clan.

The Command Sargeant Major knew we had mass casualties, which for me consisted of thirty-seven hours with no sleep the day before Westy's inspection. Captain King also told us not to come to surgery, because she wanted us rested from our previous duty since she did not know what to expect the next day.

I informed her that Tops (CSM) had issued a standing order stating everyone would fall out for police call at revelry at 5:30 a.m. This was a standard stateside program. (For the reader, everyone fell in for morning revelry.) "Police call" meant pick up any item that did not move to assure the area was ready for the Full Field Layout of all an individual's equipment. For sure, it allowed no mud on your tent pegs, although we stood in our jungle boots ankle-deep in mud.

The US Army program wanted to keep each soldier snapped in. We did this "police call" daily at each military base. At Fort Polk, Louisiana, I received my first introduction to this way of life during boot camp. And we were in peacetime back then.

Fast forward to 1966 when I was in a Vietnam jungle, War Zone D, trying to live. I preferred to make it out of there alive and in one piece while saving as many of the poor soldiers alongside me as possible.

Captain King, decision maker, gave me and two other technicians orders to disregard reporting to Sgt. Major's mandatory "police call." She assured us she would discuss it with him. The captain must have forgotten, because CSM was not informed.

When CSM awakened me, he completely turned over my rack, entangling me in my mosquito net bar.

It broke, and he hollered at me to fall out for the police call. I could fill more than one page with explicit words I called him. All my pent-up emotions—the months of anger—erupted on him. CSM continued to holler for me to stand down or be court marshaled under the articles of war.

I remember telling him, "Please do it. Court martial me. And in the court martial, include orders so I'm sent to Vietnam."

He said, "I've had enough of your BS attitude and disobeying orders. Get your web gear and steel-pot helmet and follow me to the orderly room."

Tops gave the soldier on duty as the CQ (Charge of Quarters) the forms to fill out for my court martial. Upon completing the forms, they were sent to Captain Green who was the Executive Officer, and he signed my court martial forms and forwarded them to Colonel Sadler.

Colonel Sadler called me into his office with the CSM in attendance. He asked if I had anything to say before he signed my court martial and handed me over to the MPs (Military Police).

I said, "Yes." Then, I shared all the information with him. Tops knew we had a mass casualty event, and Captain King was going to inform him we were excused from the police call the following morning.

Colonel Sadler instructed me to wait in the orderly room. He sent a CQ runner to get Captain King from the mess hall for the meeting. Captain King arrived, and I was called back into Colonel Sadler's office. She validated what I told him earlier.

Then Colonel Sadler said, "If I hear your name again in my command, I won't put you in the stockade. I'll put you under it. Do you understand that?"

"Yes, sir."

"Dismissed."

I saluted and smirked as I walked past the CSM on the way out.

Within two weeks, the entire 173rd Brigade moved. Our hospital shut down and was sent to the Mekong Delta to prepare for the arrival of the 9th Infantry Division. The complete medical staff was ordered to different MASH units except for me. I had requested being sent to the hospital in Saigon to work where all patients with brain injuries were taken. Approximately a week later, there was nothing left but the motor pool, and Tops (CSM) wanted to see me since he had my orders.

As I walked into the orderly room, Tops was smiling with his boots on the desk and handed me my orders with a big smile. I read the orders. I was attached to the 68th Medical Group for the 9th Infantry Division as a convoy driver. That meant driving 160 miles round trip twice a week to the 9th Infantry Division to bring new troops and a water tank. I told CSM I was going to Brigade to dispute and fight those orders.

He laughed and said they came from Brigade. Since he was a lifer dog soldier, he had a lot of influence. Many stories about the months from December 1966 to May 1967 remain in my memory. I will divulge more of my 1966 Merry Christmas in another story.

As a sidebar… no one wanted to even think about being a convoy driver, so we kept failing the test. Believe it or not, Colonel Pixley put out a "general order." Any soldier failing the driver's test three times consecutively would be given an Article 15 with a $300 fine and reduced one grade in rank.

Needless to say, things didn't go well. That began my convoy driving as a medic. I still didn't see God in any of this, but He was always there.

Merry Christmas 1966

Yet another holiday "stand down" from my 4th of July 1966 arrival and my 20th birthday, October 2, 1966. We learned the U.S. Army rhetoric. We would honor their holidays, and they (the Viet Cong and North Vietnam soldiers) would honor ours. What a load of BS. On Christmas 1966, they attempted to blow up our mess hall during breakfast.

Merry Christmas morning to us. Another story I will pave over at this time.

I was snapped into driving in the convoys twice a week. The vehicles were still being inventoried at the motor pool, because they were left behind when the 173rd moved away. After each convoy, as the driver and designated owner of a two-and-a-half ton truck, I had the responsibility for all maintenance. My drill was to see to all the requirements for the truck being always ready for the standing order, "Move out."

Again, I had another a-hole first sergeant from the previous wars as my shotgun (passenger seat) in the lead truck. Since I began this program of punishment around November 1, 1966, I had worked my way up to being the number-one "lead truck for all the convoys." The only positive benefit of that position was I didn't have to eat the dust like all the poor drivers behind me, and the last truck driver really caught hell.

"Sometimes," we had a tank behind every tenth truck. I never knew how long the convoy was until the other units arrived in the staging area and headed down the same road leading to the Delta. The 114-degree temperature with a steel pot (helmet), flak jacket, and pair of goggles felt like roasting in a hot oven. I have not decided to this day which one was my worst fear—the bridges that were falling in from the overweight trucks and tanks or the snipers. The enemies' protocol was to take out the first and the last truck, because they were a sure bet, and it brought the convoy to a halt.

On one of my many drives to and from the Mekong, the snipers took out three guys from the third truck. We figured it had to be two snipers to get three of us at the same time. But for some reason, they hit the third truck, not my lead one. As always, it seemed like forever before the "napalm" dropped, lighting up the tree line so we could move forward to the Fire Base for the 9th Infantry.

Despite seeing death so near, I didn't think much about God, but He was always there.

Henry Fonda—1966
Republic of South Vietnam

TODAY STARTED LIKE SO many others, waiting for the "autoclave five" call sound for the medivacs to bring in the wounded. Still attached to the 3rd MASH, I was unaware my days of living on this firebase were numbered. (Numbered because of my mental attitude.)

Then I heard the CQ runner (change of quarters) shout as he crossed our compound, "Henry Fonda wants to shake your hand."

We were told Henry was at the edge of our compound by the 3rd Chopper Pad, which was the landing pad for the "dust offs" (helicopter ambulances). Not everyone was courteous as I was, even though we all knew his daughter was a traitor to our cause. Jane even had our POWs in Hanoi punished for passing info to her they hoped she would smuggle to our side. Instead, she gave all the information to the North Vietnamese. I call that treason, with tried-and-true reasons to call her a traitor in my eyes. I have often pondered if she had been one of my daughters, would I see her as her dad did. He felt compelled to fly 10,000 miles plus and make apologies for her actions. Fifty years later, I still believe Jane's actions were treasonous.

As I walked up to Henry Fonda, he reached out to me for a handshake, thanking me on behalf of the American people for the job I was doing. He added I had his full support in serving our country during this time of war.

He explained. "I am not in agreement with what my daughter, Jane, is doing. But she is still my daughter. Maybe one day, if you ever have a daughter, you can understand that whatever she did, she would still be your daughter."

Henry brought a cameraman to take our picture together if a soldier wanted. I took the picture with him, and fifty years later, even though it faded, I still have it. I still have very mixed emotions about his pleas to forgive Jane and her actions. First, I have to remember the 58,400-plus brothers and sisters that died for her and another 200,000-plus seriously wounded. Did she have the right to support our enemy? No!

Today, I have two daughters, and at 79, my answer is still no, whether it's Jane or my daughters.

With fading memories, just like the fading picture of me and Henry, through the eyes of this medic, she truly committed an act of "treason" to the United States of America. Also, never forget the traitors who ran to Canada committed treason of a different degree.

Perhaps one day, God will help me forgive them. However, God saw it all as He wept for so many fallen soldiers in Vietnam, even if I didn't see Him.

God in Vietnam?

WHEN I TURNED 20 on October 2, 1966, I had been in country (the Nam) since July 4, 1966. On the firebase, we had access to our sleeping facilities called "hooches," which had tin roofs and screened sides. Generators created all our electricity. Despite the screened sides, we slept under mosquito nets as an extra layer of protection. The unrelenting, insatiable insects carried the possibility of malaria and other diseases.

Rats ran across the wooden bars throughout the night, taunting us with their sheer size. Even cats and dogs (though rare on our firebase) kept their distance from the oversized rodents.

At dusk, all generators turned off. No need to light the way for our enemy, including the dreaded mosquitoes. Rats, unfortunately, didn't need any light to forage around the camp or our hooches.

Before lights out at night, several of the guys read their Bibles. With my childhood history of

Catholicism, God didn't look like anything I wanted. If God even existed, I believed He was not working for me. He never seemed to care about me during my childhood, so why would He care about me as a young adult in such a terrible war? Nam solidified these doubts about Him.

I classified myself at the time as being agnostic. Maybe God existed. But how anyone could believe He cared about people in general, or them personally, I had no clue.

Each evening, I joined several other guys, laughing at these individuals who faithfully read their Bibles. They ignored us, but we came to the conclusion that God could not be in Vietnam. How could a supposedly loving God allow us to face such day-to-day survival in a living hell, and the sin and destruction surrounding us?

At 79, I look back at my foolishness. Those of us who laughed saw the faithful few as foolish, but they knew what we didn't. God was there in Nam, and He still exists today—not only in Vietnam, but everywhere. Unbound by time or space. He is very real, loving me and allowing me to share this small bit of my history.

When I consider that time, I know He had His hands on me during my tour of duty in 1966-67. Men fell beside me. Bullets whizzed past my head, so loud they buzzed in my ears. Surely one would hit me, and I'd go down with my buddies. But somehow, they missed, and I kept standing when I could have been blown up or riddled with bullets or shrapnel like many others. I know now, He never stopped working to reveal the light despite my dark life and history of doing "my will."

Today, as a much less foolish man, I attempt to stay out of His way. I am blessed to help others find His light by praying for God to remove the "scales" from their eyes.

No God in Vietnam during the war? The least foolish men there saw Him, and despite our ridicule, they remained faithful, pointing the way. And I suspect, praying we might see the God they knew personally.

My First New Car—Plymouth Satellite

Coming back from Nam, I had obtained the rank of Sergeant E5 and the pay scale to complement the rank. With base pay, combat pay, and proficiency pay, I received as much as a South Vietnamese major—$500 a month. We had no need for money in Nam. A soldier caught with US currency meant an instant court martial. We could only use MPC (military pay script).

Before I left the Fort Ord military base, I opened a savings account and had my military pay sent directly to the bank monthly. I kept $25 each month for cigarettes and miscellaneous items at the Field Post Exchange.

Returning May 27, 1967, I planned on waiting almost five months until I turned 21 and could sign for a driver's license in the State of Louisiana. My sperm donor (father) snapped me in mentally at a very young age about driving and driver's license. He would not let me have a driver's license until I was old enough to sign for myself. He also made it clear I would never drive any car of his. Ironic considering my driving record while serving in the military.

I waited with anticipation for my 21st birthday on October 2, 1967. Before my birthday, the sperm donor said he would sign for me to get my driver's license. Shocked, I wondered why, but I sure didn't ask.

The day came for me to test for my license. As I filled out the necessary forms, the Louisiana highway patrolman made a comment that he was going to check my records. He didn't believe I was months from being 21 and didn't have a driver's license.

The sperm donor pulled out the divorce papers, showing he had full custody of me, and swore I never got a driver's license in any state.

I told the patrolman that while in the military I drove everything from sedans to two-and-a-half ton trucks.

The officer looked at me. "It doesn't count that you drove vehicles in the military."

"I know. That's why I didn't write it on the application."

I passed the driving test with 100, less a penalty for having my elbow out the window.

In Nam, we talked often about what we would do when we got back to the land of the big PX. I always claimed I was going to buy myself a new Pontiac. With a new driver's license and money available in the San Francisco bank, I set out to purchase my dream car—a Pontiac GTO.

Unaware at the time, driver's insurance cost almost $2,000 a year for those of us under 25 who wanted one of those cars. State Farm Insurance left me considering how much I wanted a GTO.

At a local dealership, I stared at the $5,000 sticker price on a new GTO. I had money, but not that much. As an alternative, I looked at a used Chevrolet Chevy II. The salesman assured me it was in great shape, declaring a grandmother purchased it for her grandson to drive back and forth to the local college. I had no reason to doubt him.

Either the salesman was a complete moron, who knew nothing about cars, or he flat-out lied to me. The vehicle completely fell apart within six months. The grandson, or someone before him, trashed out the transmission and engine, leaving me with a genuine piece of junk.

The sperm donor, a big fan of Chrysler Marquees, set it up for me to buy a new car. I drove off the lot with a brand-new gold, 1967 Plymouth Satellite, totally stripped of any extras. No air conditioning or power anything. I wanted the Plymouth Road Runner but could not afford it with zero credit history and a hefty minimum down payment through Chrysler finance. Although the sperm donor set up the purchase, I never knew his reasoning behind the sudden desire to help. He never did anything like that before, and I didn't dare ask for more, unsure of his angle. On my own, I got what I could afford, not wanting to owe the old man any favors.

Once I had my new car, which didn't break down all the time, I could do my job better. My duties included traveling as an engineer assistant for the Louisiana State Board of Health (LSBH) to inspect septic tank systems before they were covered up and new waterline grades put in the new subdivisions. I also tested the water by taking samples to the lab in downtown New Orleans.

One morning, heading to work after having the car only three months, an inattentive driver rear-ended me. The trunk flew into the back seat, but neither of us had any injuries. I took the car back to the dealer, and they repaired it with Bondo (a fix-all for accidents like that).

About one month later, on a Saturday morning, I pulled in to fill up my gas tank. The lady in front of me was filling up and had a car full of Girl Scouts. When she finished, she put her car in reverse, and put my front bumper into my radiator. Not even a year old yet, my car already had the front and back pummeled—and not because of me, the young driver.

To aggravate the situation, she lied about the insurance company claim and gave me false information. I had to locate her in the New Orleans metroplex to get my car repaired after finding her name through a cross directory. Not an easy feat, but determined, I refused to let her get away with banging up my not-so-new car.

Back on the road after more car repair with Bondo on the front end, I stopped at a Burger King on Veteran's Hwy. Unbelievably, a woman coming out of the drive-through ran smack into the right side of my car. The front passenger door took the brunt of that hit.

More Bondo, and I hit the road again with the LSBH. Looking back, I can't remember exactly when I got hit on the left side. But several months later, back at the dealer for more Bondo.

My friends and family laughed. They said I'd probably have to turn the car over to hit the hood. It was the only part not sporting a healthy dose of Bondo. I had no plans for a rollover.

In less than six months, I drove from the West Bank to the East Bank on the Huey P. Long Bridge. This bridge, built in 1925, had two lanes in each direction with the railroad running down the middle. It was nothing to drive along and have a train pass. As I crossed the bridge in my Bondo car, a massive piece of concrete blew off a concrete truck, landing on the roof of my car. I hunched down as the weight pushed in the top. Bondo repair number five! Less than two years old, that poor Satellite withstood more dents than a test car. Surely, I had enough Bondo with no part left to hit.

Sometime later, in Lafitte, Louisiana, during another LSBH inspection, I drove down a gravel road. A truck flew toward me like a man on fire. Passing without slowing down, the truck flung gravel hard and fast. He covered my front windshield with cracks, completely taking it out.

In need of a new windshield, I contacted the insurance company. Again, through no fault of mine, they made arrangements for a new windshield installation. They told me I could get a tinted windshield and pay the difference from a standard one. I liked that idea, and with it installed, I picked up my car from downtown New Orleans. Heading out to Metairie via Airline Highway, I drove under a railroad overpass. Two or more juveniles stood on the overpass and dumped two sizeable containers of oyster shells onto my new tinted windshield. Gone.

Upon reaching the office, I phoned the glass repair company and arranged for another new windshield. They didn't seem too upbeat about replacing it again. Then I backtracked the insurance company for two windshields instead of one. They were not happy for sure.

Certainly not the dream of owning a car I envisioned while in Nam—more like a nightmare of vehicle ownership. In conclusion of this incident with my first new car, I paid Chrysler Credit $800 to settle the loan on the gold Plymouth Satellite so I could purchase another car.

If I could show all this "in color," you'd probably laugh alongside my family. Looking back, I can chuckle, but I sure didn't laugh back then. And despite never suffering injuries in any of these accidents, I didn't see God in them. I suspect He hovered nearby, wondering with a chuckle how much it'd take for me to see Him.

Herman The Rat

ABOUT TWO MONTHS AFTER returning from Vietnam, I rented a one-bedroom apartment above a shoe repair shop. The Margarvio family had their residence on the bottom floor, and their shoe shop was there too. This was in 1967 around November.

After being there a couple of weeks, I was lying on the floor watching TV and I caught out of the corner of my eye something hopping. I looked closer. A rat as large, if not larger, than the ones in Nam. Coal black, he stood up on his hind legs and looked at me, fearless. After a moment, he hopped back behind the refrigerator.

Around dinnertime, I went downstairs and interrupted the Margarvio's meal, asking if they had any large rat traps?

Mrs. Margarvio asked if I had seen Herman. They had been attempting to catch him for a long time but were unsuccessful. She would give me a trap but said it would be of no use since they could never catch and kill Herman.

Herman? They named this rodent as if he lived there as a pet. So I took the giant trap. I had a file for sharpening tools in the trunk of my car. Instead of heading straight upstairs, I retrieved the file and filed down the release where you place the bait. I put on a smörgåsbord of cheese and cold cuts from my refrigerator.

I went to bed and woke up about 3 a.m., grabbing my pistol and flashlight to check the trap. Nothing caught yet. When I got up for work at 6 a.m., I checked the trap first thing. I found Herman's paw in the trap. Herman lay in a pool of blood nearby. Apparently, the trap hit him on the head.

I placed his dead body in newspaper and took him and the trap down to the Margarvios, who were having breakfast, and showed them the lifeless Herman.

They seemed mesmerized by how I had done it. After enduring all the rats in Nam, no way would I stand by and share an apartment with one in the US.

Even in such a little thing, God knew what I needed and helped me kill that rodent.

Houston

I WAS IN HOUSTON, Texas, at the Houston Branch of the Internet Company, F.C.A.—one of 85 branches worldwide. They transferred me from New Orleans where I had joined the company about two and a half years earlier. They promoted me and gave me a company car. With all expenses paid, they sent me to Houston in November 1987 with one purpose, as stated by the Regional Vice President out of Atlanta—to put out the fires.

The previous management had not performed their duties for the client base. The company was a commercial credit and collection corporation, piercing corporate umbrellas. I joined this new industry following my history of alcoholism and treatment on June 24, 1985 at the Gulfport Veterans Hospital (VA). Yes, the same hospital where the sperm donor worked for twenty-three years. God really does have a sense of humor, because He put me on the same ward with forty other veterans where the sperm donor worked—Ward D.

As the program of Alcoholics Anonymous (AA) teaches, it is imperative to find a Higher Power (a God of your understanding). For the record, I did not jump up from my sofa to see what was happening at AA. They discharged me from the hospital on June 24, 1985. I still had not pursued a higher power like the program teaches.

I had been dry drunking since my hospital discharge. AA coined this term to describe those who quit drinking but still have the issues which led them to drink. Dry drunks may relapse into alcohol or move to another addiction.

Most individuals believe (as I did) they have a drinking problem, but in reality, we all have a thinking problem. The alcohol (ETOH) is a drug used as a support system, and a crutch, if you will.

I never did street drugs. For the record, I didn't use any drugs during my tour of duty as a medic in 1966-67 or in my daily life before or after the war. To this day, I cannot understand the troops that did. When I served, we were very disciplined and followed the chain of command—definitely not the place to be using drugs. Nevertheless, one must understand alcohol is a drug—albeit a legal one.

ETOH abuse is a term for excessive drinking that can lead to alcohol use disorder. ETOH stands for ethyl alcohol or ethanol. Yeah. The same type of alcohol used in mixed drinks is used in solvents, antiseptics, and gasoline although with other additives of course.

When I returned from my tour of duty on May 27, 1967, I could not express how numb I was to life. Not to mention the anger I had to deal with and more serving. My discharge came after four years with two years left to serve in a supposedly non-active reserves unit.

However, I experimented with marijuana but did not like or enjoy it. Marijuana made me more paranoid because it was illegal. I held a deep fear of the legal system because of my arrest on three counts of aggravated assault (I was very sober at 3:15 a.m.) in June 1970. Employed in upper management, I feared any involvement with this street drug. If I purchased the illegal drugs while in our car and got caught, who would take care of my two daughters? At that time, they were two and four.

I didn't see God's hand in the paranoia, but perhaps it kept me from becoming addicted to drugs instead of alcohol.

God was in Houston with me. He was always there even if I couldn't see Him.

Shana's Illness

ON AN OCTOBER AFTERNOON, 1988, at approximately 2 p.m., I received a phone call from my daughter's mother, Linda M. She sounded hysterical, crying and her voice cracking. She told me Shana (our six-year-old daughter) had been in a coma since around 7 a.m. The doctors had given up on raising her body temperature from under 93 degrees to a normal temperature of 98.6 degrees. This had already happened to Shana at six months old, but her recovery that time happened overnight.

This time, the doctors tried everything, but they did not think she would live through the night. They suggested we accept it and move forward with planning her funeral arrangements.

As my office secretary sought airline tickets to Fort Worth from the Houston Hobby Airport, no flights showed up. She finally found a ticket to the Dallas-Fort Worth International Airport, leaving at 5 p.m.

I had not had a drink since treatment on June 24, 1985. On October 8, 1988, as the plane lifted off the runway, I was at the point of relapse. Over three years of recovery from my time as a dry drunk. An overwhelming desire for a triple scotch whiskey and water to calm my nerves and mental pain hit me. Through divine intervention (I have no idea why except through a loving God), the scales fell from my eyes. For the first time, I thought of praying, and I asked the stewardess to keep my glass full with club soda.

However, as I sipped my drink, I attempted the prayers I knew from my childhood—like the Hail Mary, Glory Be, and Our Father. Most importantly, I prayed with total honesty. I told God that if He was real and did not take my baby girl, I would forever seek His face. I promised to do His will for my remaining time of living one day at a time. As an alcoholic, I knew no other way to live. During that flight, I lived from one club soda to the next, and God heard my prayers.

From my birth, the sperm donor programmed me to believe that in life only one God existed—that was the Catholic God. Nothing about a relationship with Father God through Jesus Christ, but a warped sense of this man's God.

I grew up as an altar boy and had to learn Latin. Today, I believe this was his way to have everyone (family and friends) believe we were the perfect family.

We were so far away from being the ideal family, to say the least. His idea of following God confused me—what an understatement.

But on the plane that day, I reached out to the True God instead of relying on rote prayers that meant little to me. The despair and pain of a father's heart found the God who understood losing a child more than I could imagine.

Throughout my life, Jesus never left my side. He brought me through Vietnam, stood beside me during the many years of drinking and poor decisions, and I never saw Him. As the plane flew toward DFW Airport, He sat beside me, holding my hand and assuring me of His presence. And for the first time, I knew He was there—with me and with my precious daughter.

The doctors missed it. Shana didn't die that night, and I experienced rebirth.

In His Hands

October 24, 2024

After over 60 years, I know for a fact that a Higher Power (God) definitely protected my life.

I have so many feelings of freedom today that I'm unable to describe with words. But I know anyone reading this book can have these feelings, too. I'm not selling anything. This is my testimony of "true freedom," and it is available to you and anyone who has what I call the "want to." (The "want to" is your willingness to seek His face and love.)

Back in 1966, my Catholicism did nothing to help me cope with the evil side of the war! After two or three months, we realized we were victims of the US government. But at eighteen, we did not know about "follow the money" with good old Uncle Sam. To top things off, we realized the military gave us orders to follow from Washington D.C., but the powers in D.C. did not want to win the war.

Maybe you could arrive home with your entire body intact—except chunks of your mind or emotions might be shredded. Maybe we lost the ability to "love" because as a medic, you cannot save everyone. Some soldiers got blown away. Just another body—if any parts remained for the body bags or a poncho when all the body bags were gone.

We sent the remains to "Graves Registrar" for them to process and send back to the loved ones. Understandable that on a typical night in the hooch, before the generators shut down, the guys who believed in Jesus read their Bibles. They read for comfort, peace, and hope.

Guys like myself agreed to tell them there was no God in our situation (the Nam). We told them God might be in Hawaii or Canada, but to us he was TDY (transferred to another duty station).

To complement the heat and rice rats running across our mosquito bars, which hung over our racks, we listened to the one radio station in Saigon. They played the broadcaster Hanoi Hannah as we lay in the dark and listened to current information about the baby births, announced for guys. The American Red Cross would confirm the births the next day, provided no mortar or short-run rocket fell in the compound. We wondered how Hanoi Hannah knew before the American Red Cross. She didn't broadcast to encourage the troops but did her best to spread propaganda and discourage soldiers.

While we lay in the dark, we also listened to the 319th artillery as they fired their 155s every hour. New arrivals, they tagged us the FNGs (Frigin New Guys). I learned they were firing for H&I (Harassment and Interdiction—military action impeding the enemy). Basically, we counted the time between their hourly firing as quiet and peaceful.

However, waiting for the sounds of the dust-off helicopter with the wounded and dying was always at the forefront of our minds. For me, just another day in the Nam. My duty was as a soldier first, medic second, and I was getting further away from "the order of the day." Number one, know your enemy, and number two, send the dead enemy body count for the day to General Westmoreland and the brass in Saigon.

We were there for God, Duty, Country, and Mom's apple pie. To me, every day felt like a year. I often wondered how the traitors in Canada were resting and enjoying the desertion of their flag and country.

Despite my feelings about the war in general, I couldn't abandon the duty to my country. Although I may not have felt much toward the duty to God, if I only looked for Him, I would have found Him there. Those men with their Bibles knew, and I could have asked them. But I didn't want to know, because I only knew about God. I didn't know Him. Somehow, He knew me. And I'm eternally grateful He did.

My Daily Strive to Survive

and not Become a Victim

THE FOLLOWING LINES ARE to bring my tour of duty and my life stories to a close.

On my day to get a spot on "The Freedom Bird," which had 212 seats, it happened to be the same type of plane that brought me and other soldiers into the country of Vietnam on July 4, 1966. That day, The Freedom Bird was taking me back to the land of the Big PX USA, for my four-year discharge at the Oakland Army Terminal in California.

Driving the convoys twice a week, which averaged 80 miles from War Zone D to the Mekong Delta, made each day seem like a year. The snipers were many and very accurate.

One morning, when I was driving the lead truck, snipers took out three soldiers in the third truck. Which caused us to assume there must have been two snipers on those kill shots. Almost nightly, the Viet Cong, an aggressive enemy, launched constant mortar and rocket attacks on the firebase for the 9th Infantry Division. The North Vietnamese were very upset, because we found their command center almost 40 miles from the capital in Saigon.

As I look back, I can appreciate the daily grace given to me by my Savior, Jesus. I lived for so many years without belief in a power greater than myself. I lived with a doubtful, agnostic mindset. However, today, I live my life knowing something or someone was covering my defects of character. I understand the difference between being in bondage compared to the true freedom of understanding given to me by my God and Lord Jesus.

In closing, please understand that "free will" is a life choice. And never forget, "Everything has a price." I've learned that the choice of making wise decisions equals a great life, and our bad decisions... Well, we all know what happens with that.

May God keep you in His grip for all who want a true freedom experience daily with God's grace so freely given as a "gift."

PAPAY

References

KEN-1695, THOMAS. 1737. "Now I Lay me Down to Sleep." In New England Primer, by Thomas Fleet. Thomas Fleet.

About the author

Charley J. LaFontaine

With a background of an abusive and alcohol drenched childhood, Charley J. LaFontaine voluntarily enlisted to fight in the Vietnam War. After one tour of duty, serving as a medic and in other positions, he returned to the United States and promptly denied his military service. Although he became a successful businessman, Charley carried a hidden secret—an unrelenting desire for alcohol. He became a functional alcoholic. But that's not the end of his story.

Charley found healing through a personal relationship with Jesus Christ and overcame his addiction to alcohol. He went on to eventually become a champion for fellow veterans struggling with addiction. While he's not proud of many elements of his past, Charley gives credit to the Lord for his recovery and strives to help others overcome addictions—especially those who use them to deal improperly with PTSD.

The author lives in Granbury, Texas with his wife, Blanche and is quick to admit a poignant truth. "Jesus was always there in my life—even when I didn't see him. As far as I can tell, He is the only way to overcome addictions."

Endnotes

1. (Ken-1695 1737)

www.ingramcontent.com/pod-product-compliance
Lightning Source LLC
Chambersburg PA
CBHW050758150726
48196CB00049B/1211